Letters to Marcia

A Teacher's Guide to Anti-Racist Education

Letters to Marcia

A Teacher's Guide to Anti-Racist Education

Enid Lee

Cross Cultural Communication Centre

2909 Dundas Street West
Toronto, Ontario M6P 1Z1

1992 PRINTING

 15

Canadian Cataloguing in Publication Data

Lee, Enid
    Letters to Marcia: a teacher's guide to anti-racist education

Includes bibliographical references
ISBN 0-9691060-5-X.

1. Race relations - Study and teaching.   2. Racism - Study and teaching.   3. Race relations in school management.   4. Intercultural education.   I. Cross Cultural Communication Centre (Toronto, Ont.).   II. Title.

HT1506.L43 1985   370.19'342   C85-098377-0

Design and Illustration:	Margie Bruun-Meyer
Editing:	Barb Thomas
Production:	Art Work
Typesetting:	Action Print
Printing:	Action Print
Publisher:	Cross Cultural Communication Centre
Cover photo:	Margie Bruun-Meyer

FOREWORD

Dear Colleagues

Letters to Marcia is an important first, a book of thoughtful concerns and practical activities to assist Canadian educators in furthering anti-racist education. It does not assume what the reader knows, but is designed to allow each educator to start it at her or his own entry point. Nor does it presume to have all the answers, though it certainly presents the direction for asking the right questions.

"Anti-racist education ... is just good education." That is the theme of this book. It must become the foundation of education if Canada's goal of multiculturalism is to be achieved. Anti-racist education will meet the needs of all students in Canada's schools, while preparing young people to help create an equitable society and a viable future.

Enid Lee has long been a model of what a concerned and committed individual educator can achieve within the educational system as an advocate for good education for *all* children. She has a demonstrated ability of working with teachers — individually, in workshops and in courses — to bring out the best. Her style is non-threatening yet honest. She makes people comfortable with sharing concerns, analyzing situations and exploring strategies for change, empowering others to overcome problems that block effective teaching. Enid Lee has been an inspiration for the many educators with whom she has collaborated. With *Letters to Marcia*, she shares her skills and insights in a format that can assist many more to achieve good education for all students.

Best Wishes,

Teresa González
Supervisor of Affirmative Action
and Race Relations,
Metropolitan Separate School Board
Toronto

Robert Moore
Former Resource Director,
Council on Interracial Books for Children,
New York City

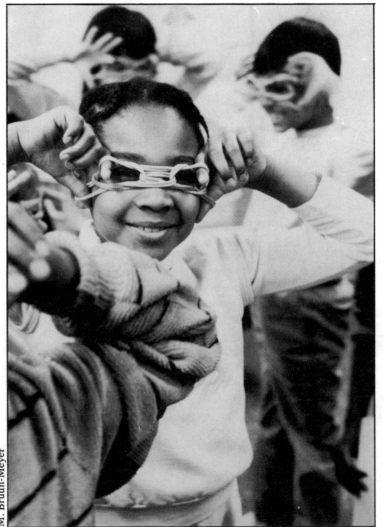

ACKNOWLEDGEMENTS

Many students, teachers, colleagues and friends have contributed to the development of this book with their experiences, analysis and words of encouragement. Their names would fill the book if I were to list them all. In a sense they do fill the book for so many of my insights have come from them. I would especially like to thank the following people:

In particular:
Barb Thomas, Educator and Writer for her unswerving optimism that the book would be completed; for numerous hours of discussion and analysis; for shaping and editing and all the countless "special effects" which she contributed to the delivery process that brought this book into being.

For classroom examples:
Bernice Blackman, Educator.
Liz Coelho, Educator.
Gloria Williams, Educator.

For encouragement, sustained interest and critical comments:
Mutale Chanda, Member of Book Advisory Committee.
LeRoy Cox, Community Organizer and Writer.
Marcela Duran, Multicultural Consultant.
Teresa Gonzalez, Supervisor-Affirmative Action, Metropolitan Separate School Board.
Ken Gould, Program Leader, Heritage Languages, Board of Education for the City of North York.
Kathy Le Blanc, Educator.
Natalie Little, Educator.
Hugh McKeowen, Supervising Principal, Heritage Languages and Race and Ethnic Relations, Board of Education for the City of North York.
Marlene Philip, Writer.
Jeff Piker, Member of Book Advisory Committee.
Odida Quamina, Educator.
Susan Roy, Member of Book Advisory Committee.
Jon Young, Research Consultant.

For suggesting the concept "Letters To Marcia:"
Marcia Ziskind, Educator.

For opportunities to work with teachers:
Alba Falconi, Consultant, Immigrant Studies, Peel Board of Education.
Teresa Gonzales, Supervisor — Affirmative Action, Metropolitan Separate School Board.
Jean Handscombe, Co-ordinator, English as a Second Language/Dialect, Board of Education for the City of North York.
Tony Souza, Former Advisor on Race Relations, Toronto Board of Education.

For the opportunity to write the book:
Personnel and Program Committee of the Cross Cultural Communication Centre.
The Staff and Board of the Cross Cultural Communication Centre.

For inspiration in anti-racist work:
Robert Moore, Former Resource Director of Interracial Books for Children.

For cheerfully typing drafts:
Dorothy Thompson, Educator.
Beulah Worrell, Typist.

For her artistic interpretation of ideas and for capturing the spirit of school life with her camera:
Margie Bruun-Meyer, Artist.

For permission to take photographs in their school:
Wayne Calver; principal, Bathurst Heights.
Bill Hogarth; principal, Shoreham Public School.
Bob Lawson; principal, Oakwood Collegiate.
Ian McLellan; Vice Principal, A.Y. Jackson.
And all the students and staff who participated with such grace and enthusiasm.

For help locating photographs on pages 13, 27, 31 and 33:
Mudpie Magazine.

For financial support:

The Government of Canada, through the Secretary of State Multiculturalism Director-
    ate.
The government of Ontario through the Ontario Ministry of Citizenship and Culture.
Atkinson Charitable Foundation.
The volunteer fund-raisers of the Cross Cultural Communication Centre.

M. Bruun-Meyer

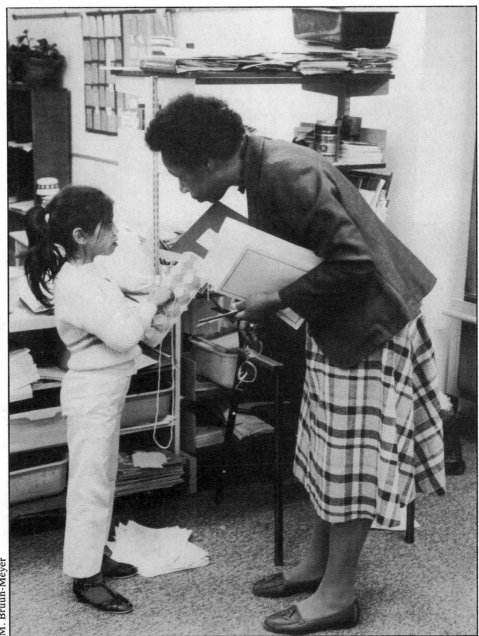

CONTENTS

DAY 4

8:45-8:55   Home Room Supervision
8:55-9:00   Announcements

Introduction

9:00-9:50   Period One   7H/7E History

Chapter I

9:50-10:40   Period Two   7E English

Chapter II

10:40-11:30   Period Three   7H English

Chapter III

11:30-12:50   Period Four   Guidance Office

Chapter IV

12:50-1:40   Period Five   Project Planning

Conclusion

INTRODUCTION

M. Bruun-Meyer

Dear Colleagues,

In preparing this guide, I thought of some of you who trusted me and allowed me to look over your shoulders at your struggles with Canada's multicultural/multiracial reality in your classrooms. I recalled also, the numerous exchanges I have had with others of you in workshops and Faculty of Education courses. The experiences recorded here come from you. I trust that they will have some relevance to teachers in classrooms in a wide variety of settings, for this guide is intended for all teachers.

I have attempted to identify some of the situations which you face in your daily work in order to demonstrate how inequities based on race and sometimes

on ethnicity, gender and class can function in a
school. But I have also provided information,
analysis and activities which can enable you to use
these very situations to contribute to anti-racist
education in all areas of school life.

This letter is one of six you will find in this
book. The idea of using letters came from a teacher
named Marcia after I had helped her to identify some
unexplored potential in her students over a number
of weeks. She suggested that we continue to share our
insights on multicultural/multiracial education through
letters. I found this idea stimulating. I saw
potential for dialogue and for building bridges of
solidarity between teachers in various parts of the
country as we struggle to provide education which is
liberating for us and for our students, and by exten-
sion, for the whole society.

Some activities in schools are designed to main-
tain order, but there are others with the distinct
potential for changing the order and making it more
equitable. Writing can be viewed as one such activity.
I hope that the contents of this guide will generate
thoughts and actions which you will share in writing
with colleagues in many places.

Sincerely,

Enid

HOW TO USE THIS GUIDE

Orientation

Before you turn to the activities in the middle of the book, let me encourage you to read the first chapter, *Anti-Racist Education: What's It All About?*, for it provides a necessary orientation for the anti-racist activities you will find in this guide. In addition, this first chapter will probably address some of the concerns you may have on the subject of race, culture, and education.

Format

Each of the remaining chapters contains four sections. Each is organized around situations with which you are familiar in your daily practice. You will find the following sections in Chapters 2, 3, and 4: a letter; staff development notes and activities; classroom activities; and resources. Each of these sections may be used independently although a chapter used in its entirety would allow a staff and several classes in a school to engage simultaneously in anti-racist activities.

Focus

In Chapters 2, 3, and 4, three related aspects of school life are explored: community, curriculum, and support services for students. These are concerns for all educators. However, Chapter 2 is important for both classroom teachers and administrators; Chapter 3 is especially directed to classroom teachers; and Chapter 4 is of particular interest to administrators and guidance counsellors, and all those who provide support services.

Letters

The letter in each chapter is integrated into the staff development and classroom activities and it provides a case study and an analysis of how racism is produced. The case contained in each letter can be used for discussion independently of the rest of the chapter.

Activities — Integrative Possibilities

The activities for both staff development, and for classroom use, are not meant to be **additional** curriculum. You are encouraged to integrate them into your existing program and they may eventually influence your other activities. The activities cut across Language and Social Studies, and are aimed at assisting students in developing a critical approach to social issues, and in engaging in action to change unjust situations.

Resources: Audiovisual and Human

Most of the audiovisual material is available at the National Film Board offices. You are urged to draw on the human resources in your area in order to bring an immediate perspective to the discussion of race and racism. Multicultural and Race Relations Departments, Ministries of Culture, Church Groups, Community Groups and activists, International Students' Clubs at universities, Heritage Language teachers, Cultural Centres, Human Rights Offices are good sources for resource people.

1 ANTI-RACIST EDUCATION: What's It All About?

M. Bruun-Meyer

"If racism could have been eradicated, it would have been by now."

Grade 11 Student

Dear Marcia,

    This letter, like all the others in this book,
deals with an uncomfortable topic - Racism. It is an
uncomfortable topic for many respectable, well-meaning
Canadians. Raising the topic might be compared to
breaching a code of conduct. Some of us even believe
that the more we talk about racism the worse it becomes.
The implication is that if we don't talk about it, it
will go away. On the contrary, if we talk about
racism, we begin to understand it. Informed talk
about racism is like good health education. If for
example we learn how the teeth decay, what kinds of
food and activities lead to a toothache, then we know
to care for our teeth. In the same way when we learn
how racism works, and what forms it takes, then we can
do something about creating anti-racist schools.

    You must be wondering where anti-racist education
fits in with the hundreds of other requirements that
are laid on to teachers.   The burden will be
lightened if we recognize that anti-racist education
points the way to a sound and equitable education for
students of all races and cultures.

    One of the assumptions which undergirds this work
is that racism can be unlearned. Research into the
nature of racism and into the learning process enables

us to support our claim. Unlike the student who said, "if racism could have been eradicated it would have been eradicated," we do believe that racism can be eradicated. You will find here some questions and information which should serve as tools in combatting racism.

After you have read it all you will probably say "What do these activities have to do with racism? They just make for good education and should be available to all of our students". If you say that, then I know that I will have made myself clear, for anti-racist education is not special or compensatory education, it is just good education. Thanks for listening and providing me with new questions.

Sincerely,

Enid

SO WHAT DOES ANTI-RACIST EDUCATION HAVE TO DO WITH YOU?

In Anticipation.....

Perhaps you are wondering whether to read these *Letters to Marcia*. They deal with Anti-Racist Education. You are no racist; your colleagues are good decent people who want only the best for their students and yours is not a racist school. No racial violence in your school; kids of all races play happily together; and you have organized several days when you celebrate food, festivals and folklore from other lands. No this book really isn't for your school. No need for anti-racist education here........

And you teach in a mainly white school. There are very few students from other cultures and they seem very comfortable. You hardly ever hear the word "race" mentioned. Very little chance of racism here. Of course you teach units on Canada's Native people and the various peoples who have settled in Canada over the years, so you know that your students have good attitudes to peoples of all cultural backgrounds. No need for anti-racist education here......

For the past decade you have tried to introduce multicultural education in your classroom, encouraging your students to celebrate cultural differences and to recognize similarities. Mutual respect and tolerance — these have been your watchwords. What has happened to good old multicultural education? Why do we need anti-racist education? Probably some import from the United States or Britain. No relevance to Canada. No need for anti-racist education here......

In Response

Anti-racist education is a perspective that permeates all subject areas and school practices. Its aim is the eradication of racism in all its various forms. Anti-racist education emerges from an understanding that racism exists in society and, therefore, the school, as an institution of society, is influenced by racism.

Anti-racist education attempts to equip us as teachers, and our students, with the analytic tools to critically examine the origins of racist ideas and practices, and to understand the implication of our own race and our own actions in the promotion of, or struggle against, racism. It provides us with the skills to work collectively to combat racism. It shows the relationship between our personal prejudices and the systemic discrimination which institutions practise on a daily basis. It enables us to see that racism is learned, and therefore, can be unlearned. It exposes the structures in society

—the ways we have organized our lives and institutions — that limit some people on the basis of their race, and advance others on the basis of their race. It points to the social ordering of people and groups as one of the major sources of racist ideas. It explores how the political, social, and economic life of a society is reinforced and shaped by our daily exposure to that life through the media, textbooks, cards, games, toys, and so on. It exposes inadequate explanations which attempt to justify and account for people's different positions in the society. It attacks the notion that if you work hard you will make it, for it raises questions about those who have worked hard and failed to make it. It does not allow the examiner to dismiss such "failure" as bad luck or inherent inferiority. Rather, anti-racist education highlights some of the human-made social structures and barriers which limit individuals and groups from improving their chances in life, despite their best efforts. Anti-racist education moves us forward to construct the true multicultural society of which we presently speak. It moves us beyond the comfortable aspect of each other's culture, the food and the festivals, to examining the more controversial dimensions of culture which have led to change, and can lead to change.

A publically stated goal of our multicultural society is equality of opportunity. Anti-racist education can help us realize that goal by the analysis it enables us to do of the real barriers to equal opportunity. It points to structures in our society and relations between the powerful and the powerless which must be changed if we are to achieve true equality of opportunity. Through anti-racist education, we come to understand that it is not because individuals act in bad faith, or are inherently unwilling to be generous to other people; but rather that historical patterns and contemporary situations give us the cue as to how we ought to treat each other. Anti-racist education identifies the value which society has placed on people of different racial groups. It exposes the benefits which some derive from these evaluations, and the opportunities others have lost. Anti-racist education, then, is the business of all teachers, in all schools.

Racism: What Does it Look Like in Schools?

We have said that racism exists in the schools because racism exists in the society. The eradication of racism becomes the task of every teacher. It affects us personally and professionally. In short, racism can actually prevent us from teaching well, for it can impair our relationships with our students; limit the knowledge we present and explore; and eventually limit children's opportunities in life. In practice, racism has something to do with all of the following:

- teachers having low expectations of students from racial minority backgrounds

- teachers teaching to those low expectations and students remaining unchallenged and becoming more disabled learners each year

- students accepting these limited visions of themselves and performing accordingly — describing themselves as problem children

- large groups of students being streamed in one particular subject area because they seem good at it, but denied the opportunity to grow and develop in other important areas

- students' experiences not seriously taken up in classes, but used as show and tell, and forgotten or omitted from the main curriculum

for example it is:

- Japanese Canadian students' view of wartime experience not matching the "objective" Canadian vision and the history teacher describing it as "nonsense". …history always told from the view of the conqueror

- Native Canadian children seeing themselves depicted as drunken Indians or noble savages

- Native Canadian children taught in English with no attention paid to home languages

- a Black child colouring her reading book in brown crayon, because no one in the book looks like her

Looking at the Whole Individual

Teachers frequently tell me that they do not see colour when they approach their students. They teach the individual child. That sounds fair enough, but I always ask, "What does that really mean? What has gone into the making of that individual?" To answer that question, we need to look at the social identities we all possess. The petals of this flower represent our social identities. They are social, because society places a value on all of these identities. For example, some geographic regions, economic classes, and races are more favoured by society than others. In other words, the social identities of some individuals provide them with greater access to opportunity than other individuals. To teach the individual child, we need to recognize these social inequities which some students face.

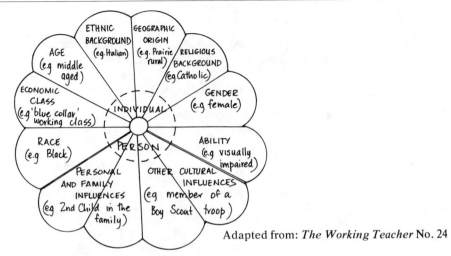

Adapted from: *The Working Teacher* No. 24

A Language Lesson

While our use of some of these words is still tentative and changing, here are some working definitions of important words used in this book.

Class — The economic, social and political relationships in which people operate in a given social order. These relationships reflect the constraints and the limitations that people experience in the areas of income level, type of occupation or sense of ownership and other markers of social rank.

Culture — Totality of ideas, beliefs, values, knowledge of a group of individuals who share certain historical experiences. Expression of culture is related to the power which groups have in the social order. Culture is dynamic and often contains elements of conflict and opposition.

Cultural forms — The symbols which express culture, e.g. music, dress, food, dance, etc. These have developed as the group attempts to make their lives out of the material and political environment.

Discrimination — The granting and/or denying of certain rights to certain groups. This behaviour results in minorities being maltreated or excluded.

Ethnic — An adjective used to describe groups which share a common language, race, religion or national group. Everyone belongs to an ethnic group. The term is often confused with ''minority''.

Institutions — Fairly stable social arrangements and practices through which collective actions are taken. Examples of institutions are government, business, unions, schools, churches, courts and police, and the people who represent the institutions.

Institutional Racism — Institutions have great power to reward and penalize. They reward by providing career opportunities for some people and foreclosing them to others. They reward as well by the way social goods are distributed—by deciding who receives training and skills, medical care, formal eduction, political influence, moral support and self-respect, productive employment, fair treatment by the law, decent housing, self-confidence, and the promise of a secure future for self and children.

One of the clearest indicators of institutional racism is the exclusion of visible minorities of society from positions of control and leadership. (From *Institutional Racism In America*, Knowles and Prewitt, Prentice Hall, 1969.)

Minority — A group with a certain set of characteristics which set it apart from the dominant group in a society—the group is usually aware of itself as having a depressed status relative to the majority and may be subjected to unequal and differential treatment. This group may be a numerical majority in world terms or even community terms.

Prejudice — A frame of mind which tends to pre-judge a person, or a group, in a negative light. This negative judgment is usually without adequate evidence. These negative attitudes are frequently not recognized as unsoundly based assumptions because of the frequency with which they are repeated. They become common sense notions which are widely accepted, and are used to justify acts of discrimination.

Race — A social category used to classify humankind according to common ancestry or descent and reliant upon differentiation by general physical characteristics such as colour of skin and eyes, hair type, stature, and facial features.

Stereotype — ''An exaggerated belief, oversimplification, or uncritical judgment about a category''. (From *The Things They Say Behind Your Back*.)

2 The SCHOOL and the COMMUNITY: How Can We Equalize the Partnership?

S. Tirimacco

"I can't tell you how many times we have invited those immigrant parents to school. They never show up. It's time they take some responsibility for their children's education."

Frustrated Teacher

Hello Marcia:

Snatches of your conversation with Mr. Singh
drifted over to where I was sitting in your room
yesterday. I gathered that he had come in to talk
about his two children who had just arrived from
Guyana. He seemed anxious to work with them at home in
order to help them catch up with the others in the
class. I'm sure you meant well when you advised him to
lay off and leave the kids to you. Did you notice his
shy, embarrassed smile when you said this? He said
nothing so you moved on to another topic.

But the incident stayed with me for a long time.
It reminded me of a conversation I had had with a
teacher who worked in a big secondary school in the
city. At a parent-teacher meeting, a Black parent
expressed the desire to help her son with Math homework. She specifically asked for the name of a Math
book to use with the boy. The Math teacher stood up
and firmly discouraged this initiative on the part of
the parent. He explained that her efforts would only
confuse the student. Further it was school policy to
leave the tutoring of students to school staff.

The parent sat down, head bowed, probably con-
vinced that she had forgotten her place. I am sure
that neither in this case nor in yours was any malice
intended. Let me share with you what I think goes
into situations like these and how I think they are
both potentially racist.

As teachers we all suffer from the need to protect
our territory. This need is produced by the tight job
market, by demands for professional identities and by
the requirements that we be specialists. Underlying
these demands are theories in educational circles that
claim children learn only what we teach them and that
there is a world of difference between people's everyday lives and the activities of academia. Alas, we
are victims of these thoughts despite our best selves.

But something else is going on here, I think.
Part of our understanding of the world is that those
school systems in other countries operate very
differently from ours. Over the years "different"
has come to mean for many of us "less" or "inadequate".
Put plainly, how could these two parents from these
poor, backward countries really know much about
education? By now, you must be ready to throttle me,
but let me finish.

The situation is complicated by the dress and
speech of both Mr. Singh and the woman at the parent
meeting. Both are making an effort to speak standard
Canadian English and they are dressed in working
clothes. Their earnest faces say they want to help
despite the hesitancy in their voices. Somehow our
notions of who they are and what they are able to do
win out over their expressed desire for parent participation -- a much-encouraged feature of Canadian
school life.

How can we avoid these situations which limit
and marginalize human beings? Maybe we could reflect
on how we might have responded to a parent who was
white, middle-class, educated and by implication able
to speak the school's language both literally and
figuratively. Having given you this earful, you are
probably wondering how you might have handled this
differently.

How can we harness parent interest, overcome
stereotypic notions about people, struggle to bring
people's everyday experiences into school life and
bridge the gulf that exists between the professional
and the lay person?

Could you perhaps have sincerely thanked Mr. Singh
for his interest and asked what specifically he had
already done to help the kids. Depending on his
answers, you might have been able to link his efforts
to the kinds of things you are doing in class. Or you
might not. For instance he might have had these two
grade five students doing hours of math problems at
night. You might have suggested that he give less work.

You would probably have gained some good insights
by inquiring whether Mr. Singh had time for leisure
activities with the children. Depending on his answer,
you might have had some additional experiences to draw
on in class. In addition you could have recommended
that he or an older relative take them to educational
places like Museums or community events or encourage

some selected T.V. viewing since these are common
reference points in your teaching. This effort would
begin to redefine the notion of homework for Mr. Singh.
Further this approach might have brought you closer to
the other's realities and provided you with an opportunity to encourage genuine parent participation.

When I said that the situation was potentially
racist, I was not implying that the situation took
place simply because Mr. Singh was not white. What
also played a part I think was Mr. Singh's social class.
He probably did not have the social and economic power
 to establish the relationship with the school which
would ensure that his experiences, his speech, and his
culture were valued. As you pointed out to me on one
occasion, our schools would function perfectly if all
our students were white and middle class. Part of the
difficulty in Mr. Singh's case is that our schools are
not geared to providing full educational opportunity
for working class, non-white parents and their children.

Let me hasten to add that I have never met a
 teacher who intends to limit a parent on the basis of
race or class or to promote feelings of inherent
inferiority in the person. However this is frequently
the result and in the final analysis, discrimination
is not so much what is intended but what is experienced.
That's all for now. I'll be in touch soon again.

Sincerely,

Enid

M. Bruun-Meyer

ENGAGING IN PARENT INTERVIEWS

Notes to the Facilitator:
Ensure that each member of the group receives a copy of the letter beforehand. If there is no opportunity for this, allow 10-15 minutes at the beginning of the session for participants to read the letter and note points for discussion.

Activities

1. Responses to the letter

List the group's responses on a flip chart. Examine the assumptions which underly their responses with respect to parents' rights, education in other countries, teachers' professional responsibilities. Several other concerns may surface, but below are some anticipated comments:

(a) "Tutoring should be left to the professionals."

(b) "The race of the parent has nothing to do with it; I have said the same thing to White parents."

(c) "It makes my work easier when parents want to be involved in their children's education."

(d) "This letter certainly challenges the view that parents from other ethnic groups don't place much value on education."

(e) "After all, they have come here. They should adapt to the school, not the other way around. Why is the school being asked to bend over backwards?"

2. Parent interviews — The Group's Experience

(a) Invite members of the group to share their experiences of parent interviews with racial minorities.

(b) List the criteria that seem to characterize both successful and unsuccessful interviews from the staff's point of view.

(c) At the end of the exploration, have the group examine and discuss the items in checklist below.

Not working at Grade level.....fine motor coordination..
...rote learning..... child centered.... Social skills....
pre voc...... abil...   ...behavioral problem.....
..environment...   ....learning disability....
acting out.....   ..educable retarded.....

CHECKLIST FOR PARENT INTERVIEWS

☐ Does the meeting time allow working parents to attend?

☐ Is the meeting in conflict with religious or cultural events in the community?

☐ Have I invited the parent to send a representative, such as an older child, if the parent is unable to attend the interview?

☐ Have I telephoned those people for whom it would be more common to convey messages orally?

☐ Have I invited translators and cultural interpreters?*

*"Cultural interpreters" are people who are familiar with the official and unofficial cultures of the school and the cultures of the home. Cultures here include the meanings, values and practices that are common not only to the ethnic group from which the parent comes but also to their social class.

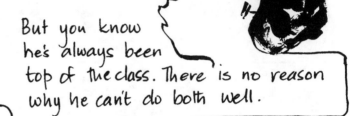

I know Harold's Math grades have dropped way down this semester. But don't be too hard on him - he did get into the basketball team!

But you know he's always been top of the class. There is no reason why he can't do both well.

☐ Do I attempt to hold some meetings with parents in the school and others in community buildings, e.g. community centres, or recreational rooms of apartment buildings?

☐ Have I ensured that the doors of the building are open so that parents can enter?

☐ Have I placed signs in appropriate languages, or appointed guides to escort parents to my room?

☐ Have support staff been made aware that members of the community will be in the school?

☐ Have I learned the correct last name and pronunciation of the parent's name?

☐ Do I have several examples of the students' work on hand?

> Will you bake cookies for Parent's Day?

> No. Not this time.

> But I will join the curriculum committee because I am concerned about stereotypes in my children's readers.

At the interview:—

☐ How specific and candid am I in giving a parent information about her child's performance?

☐ Do I believe in the student's ability to learn?

☐ Am I conveying that confidence to the parent?

☐ How clear am I at explaining what I am attempting to do in class?

☐ Am I using the opportunity to learn about the parent's hopes for his child?

☐ Am I using parents' comments to rethink my teaching strategies?

☐ Am I giving the parent a chance to ask questions?

☐ Am I listening? Am I paraphrasing and giving back to the parent my understanding of what is being said?

☐ Am I allowing time for the parent whose mother tongue is not English, or who speaks a variety of English different from mine to convey her meaning?

- [ ] Am I noting the parent's non-verbal cues?

- [ ] Am I using the opportunity to learn from the parent about the strategies which work well with the student in the area of work habits and conduct?

- [ ] Am I using the opportunity to discover ways in which the parent might contribute to the student's learning and the life of the school?

- [ ] Am I open to the fact that the parents' economic/social reality may make it impossible for them to participate in school life in the traditional ways?

- [ ] Am I using the occasion to provide a parent with more information about the school and about their rights as parents, in order to empower them to participate significantly in the life of the school?

- [ ] Am I inviting the parent to express his expectations of the school?

- [ ] Am I inviting a parent to express dissatisfactions and explore conflicts which she has experienced with the school?

- [ ] Am I using the opportunity to explain the school's race relations policy to parents from all cultural and racial backgrounds?

3. That's All Very Well.....

Having gone through the checklist, members of the group might dismiss the ideas as something which is all very well for someone who does not face the constraints which many teachers experience. First of all it is important for the group to remember that they will employ as many of these strategies as their time allows. In order to help people develop solutions, invite the group to identify the problems and outline some possible approaches to overcoming these. Discussion might look something like this:

Possible Constraints

1. No preparation time for interviews.

2. Too many parents to process in one day.

3. Time that working parents can come is inconvenient for me.

4. No access to translators.

5. No control over how support staff may treat parents.

Possible Approaches

1. Rescheduling of Professional Development days for such time. Involve active parents and/or cultural interpreters for phoning.

2. Rescheduling over a few days. Approach Federation represenative to include this item in collective bargaining so that such time be recognized as "teaching time".

3. Ask the Principal to provide compensatory time to allow you to work at an unusual hour.

4. Check Board facilities for translators. Approach a cultural group and try to secure a small honorarium from the school budget. Ensure that translators are knowledgable about dialects and familiar with the educational system.

5. Ask the Principal to discuss the issue with support staff. Suggest a workshop in which attitudes and behaviour to racial minorities are explored.

6. Unable to avoid discouraging parents when giving information about their children's performance.

6. Identify features of the student's work which are positive. Outline some of the skills and knowledge a student is expected to have in order to be functioning at relevant grade level. State concrete areas in which you are expecting student to improve.

Such discussions can not only generate ideas for reallocating existing resources and time, but may identify future demands which teachers, principals, and parents must make to ensure real dialogue between home and school. Looking squarely at constraints is often the first step to ensuring that the education system is truly serious about an issue to which it has publicly professed commitment.

M. Bruun-Meyer

REACHING OUT TO THE COMMUNITY

Activities

1. The Creation of Communities

The following are some common statements made by staff members about racial minorities.

1. "They can never agree on anything. You don't even know who their leader is. Who are their real representatives, anyway?"

2. "That group who came into the school is made up of a bunch of radicals. They don't truly represent the South Asian community. They are usually so passive and respectful."

3. "If they keep on disagreeing with each other, then the school can hardly be blamed for sitting on its hands. One really doesn't know who to follow."

4. "One of them was in school this lunch hour and I can tell you he looked just like the kind of person who would tell the kids that white teachers do not like them."

A useful approach to discussing these questions is to explore some underlying assumptions of those making the statements.

Assumption: People of racial and ethnic minorities are expected to agree on all issues.
Fact: When Anglo-Canadians disagree it is considered a diversity of opinion. With other groups, it is seen as disunity and disorganization.

Assumption: School policy is shaped largely by community pressure.
Fact: School policy frequently responds to the criteria for administrative efficiency and not community convenience.

Assumption: Institutions should deal only with those leaders who fit the image which they have of the community.
Fact: A range of leadership styles are tolerated amongst Anglo-Canadians.

Assumption: People's appearances are safe indicators of their views on race and the activities in which they will engage to convey those views.
Fact: There is frequently no correlation between appearance and views on race.

S. Tirimacco

2. Setting Standards

Prepare a set of criteria which a school could use when deciding to implement a request of educational assistance for a particular group of students. The following situation will enable you to focus on some important considerations.

A group of students originally from Laos, was experiencing difficulty comprehending some concepts in a mathematics class being taught in English. Some representatives of their community approached the Race and Ethnic Relations Department to provide the salary for a Laotian with teaching background in mathematics to give tutorials to these students in their mother tongue. The arrangements were that the students would continue to receive instructions in English during the week and be exposed to those same concepts in Laotian on the weekend. As soon as parents of children from another ethnic group heard that the the Board was funding this tutorial, they immediately requested that their children be provided with Saturday tutorials, although they were experiencing no difficulty comprehending the language of instruction. They argued that everyone should be treated alike.

A few assumptions to consider:

1. Treating everyone equally does not mean treating everyone in the same way.

2. Certain basic skills and knowledge must be in place if students are to succeed in the school system. Knowledge of the language of instruction is an important prerequisite.

3. Children from various ethnic groups differ widely in the experiences which they have had prior to coming to school. If we are to begin with where the students are, we must seriously address the experiences of each child.

4. We need to treat some students differently if we are to redress the basic inequality which is part of the education and social system.

3. Community Use of School Facilities

Assess what you know about the community-use of your school by answering the following questions collectively:

1. Do parents of children in the school use the school for community events?

2. What are the social classes, and ethnic and racial backgrounds of parents who use the school?

3. Is the school used for meetings? If so what kind — religious, cultural, political, athletic, other?

4. Which of the school facilities are community groups allowed to use if they need them for their activities (lights, stage, the kitchen).

5. How would you describe the treatment received by community groups from custodial staff? What are the characteristics of that treatment?

6. Are there nights or days when it is not possible to use the school?

7. Do more established groups in the community have long-standing arrangements to use the school?

8. What mechanism is in place to allow newer and more recent groups to gain access to the facilities?

4. Who Are the VIPs around your School?

For discussion:

A community outreach worker in one school complained of not having easy access to a phone. This makes it difficult for members of the community he serves to contact him. He claimed that if the community were perceived as politically strong and organized in the eyes of the school, then he would be treated differently. How does your school indicate to "a community" that it is important? Consider the following:

(a) How are space and equipment allocated in the school?

(b) Who has telephones?

(c) What hours are community workers expected to work?

(d) Which groups have easy access to the principal?

(e) How does the school demonstrate to students and their parents that community work is important?

ENGAGING IN PARENT INTERVIEWS

Elementary

Activities

1. Why Parents Don't Come In For Interviews

Have the students brainstorm around the issue of why parents do or do not attend parent interviews. Invite them to suggest ways in which the schools can make it more likely for their parents to attend interviews and meetings. Below are some insights from a few groups of students who have discussed this topic:

Problems	Approach
1. Parents' lives are so full of drudgery with two and three shifts in factories, that another meeting is not what they need.	1. Invite parents to attend an entertainment evening and then raise the school related issues as a secondary part of the evening.
2. The meetings are held at times when many parents are unable to attend.	2. Do a telephone survey to find out what would be the best time for parents to attend.

2. Preparing for Parents' Night

Involve the students in making a video tape of some of the activities in which they are engaged in various classes, in order to show parents what the school's program is like. The preparation would require students to write a script explaining what is done and why it is done in some classes, and to select scenes which would be video taped. For example, the activities in the English As A Second Language class could be presented in English and other languages spoken by the students. The video tape would be presented on Parents' Night. Students would have already involved their parents by telling them about the particular parts they will be presenting in this video tape.

Activities

Secondary

1. A Warm Welcome?

View either *Four Portraits* or *For What Did I Come To This Country*. Discuss with the students the experiences faced by some people in the film. How does the school help those families to feel welcome?

2. That Ugly Old Indian

That Ugly Indian

I went to the concert and dance full of confidence. Daddy had insisted that Sophie chaperone me — that was my only problem. She had on her green hood and old black coat and I was ashamed of her. But she was so proud of me that she told everyone how beautiful I was, almost as if she had invented me. During the intermission, I was standing near the door with Karen when a girl from school came over and asked loudly, "Is that woman your mother?" Everyone started to snicker and I looked at her and said, "That old, ugly Indian?": and laughed until I saw Sophie's face. She looked so rejected as she walked to a bench and sat down that I felt shame and hatred for her, myself, and the people around me. I could almost see Cheechum standing beside me with a switch saying, "They make you hate what you are."

Maria Campbell
Halfbreed

Distribute the passage entitled *That Ugly Old Indian* and discuss it. The discussion might include the following:

1. Have you ever felt ashamed of your relatives when you are in their company and you have been recognized by a friend? Explore the reasons why it did or did not happen.

2. Why do you think Maria behaved and felt as she did?

3. How would you explain Cheechum's statement, "They make you hate what you are"?

4. Do you think a school can make you hate what you are? If so, how?

5. What are some of the ways in which schools help make people feel proud of who they are?

S. Tirimacco

REACHING OUT TO THE COMMUNITY

Activities

1. Pictures of Parents

Create a collage of pictures of parents of different racial backgrounds participating in a variety of situations at home, at work, and recreation. Have the children collect pictures from magazines and, where suitable ones are not available, invite them to draw their own. Emphasize the importance of finding parents in a range of situations. Pay special attention to job stereotyping along lines of race and gender. Be sure to include a variety of family arrangements, not simply nuclear, urban middle-class. Include parents of various ages. This activity should help students become aware of their own biases in terms of racial characteristics and other aspects of social identity.

2. Parents as Teachers

Have students complete the chart below in order to demonstrate what they learned from parents. Invite parents into the classroom to act as resouce people in areas not usually associated with multiculturalism, i.e. as presenters of dances and preparers of food. In a unit on work, parents might be invited in to talk about their work. In cases where this is not possible you might conduct taped interviews with them and introduce the tapes as resources. In instances where it is possible to arrange a field trip, the class might be taken to see parents engaged in different kinds of work. They would have the opportunity to learn of the specific skills involved in the various occupations and the contributions which they make to society. In cases where work is risky and dangerous, the children should gain some insight into how and why employers do or do not protect their workers.

Elementary

	PARENTS AS TEACHERS	
Age at which I learned to do.......... or that..........	Describe the skills or the information in the space below	Name of relative

Activities

1. Parent Survey

Students develop open-ended questionnaire to determine their parents' feelings about the school. They might explore the following areas:

- Aspects of their cultural heritage which they would like included in curriculum

- Procedures for assessing and placing students

- Career Counselling

- Literacy skills in the schools

- Home work

- Discipline

- Levels of comfort in the school, e.g.:
    - treatment by receptionists, etc.
    - suitability of meeting times
    - accessibility to school administrators

Students can work in groups to develop appropriate questions around these topics. They can report back to their groups and find creative ways of sharing the findings with the rest of the class and the staff.

2. Know Your Rights

Following on the survey activity, students might develop a visually interesting hand-book on the parents' rights and responsibilities. They would need to take account of what parents coming from different countries might know about schools, especially those areas which are within their rights. On completion, students might find it appropriate to translate it into several languages.

N. Walker

Resources

Be A Good Boy Now: A Story of Displacement
16mm film 35 mins.

The scene is set in Jamaica and captures the experience of a young boy who is preparing to join his mother in Canada. We see him in school, enjoying leisure activities with his family, and we listen to his expectations for his new life in Canada. A useful resource for demonstrating the kinds of experience which some members of the West Indian community bring to the Canadian scene.
Available at the Ontario Ministry of Citizenship and Culture Resource Library.

For What Did I Come To This Country
Slide Tape Show 20 mins.

This slide tape presentation portrays the hopes and dreams of a number of people who have settled in Canada. It highlights the discrepancy between people's expectations and their experiences in Canada.
Available at The Cross Cultural Communication Centre.

Four Portraits
16mm film 28 mins. 17 secs.

Four new Canadians discuss the problems they experience in the process of immigration. They are all very optimistic about their future in Canada. A Chilean family, an Antiguan family, a young Sikh and a Russian dance master are portrayed here.
Available at the National Film Board of Canada.

Home Feelings: Struggle for a Community
16mm film 57½ mins.

This film explores aspects of life in the Jane/Finch community north of Toronto, through the eyes of some of its West Indian-Canadian residents. They describe their relations with the police, and Ontario Housing; their daily struggles with employment and unemployment; bringing up children with dignity; living in a community which is viewed negatively by outsiders; and their fragile attempts to organize their community so that residents have more of a stake in it.
Available from The National Film Board of Canada.

3 **THE CURRICULUM: How Can We Use it to Eliminate Racist Ideas?**

M. Bruun-Meyer

*"But isn't everything biased?
Besides, I'll be damned if I
stop using literature I enjoy!"*
Librarian

Dear Marcia,

I know you have been thinking a great deal about the question of bias in text books and in learning materials in general. The librarian at the public school near to you became rather upset when a workshop leader suggested the Little Black Sambo be removed from the shelves because it perpetuates racist images of the world.

The other day when I was in the school the librarian shared her concern with me. She pointed out that kids loved Little Black Sambo and that there was no harm in it. Besides, she reflected on her own liking for the story as a child. Her comments reminded me of a remark I heard at another workshop. One teacher declared, "I'll be damned if I stop using literature that I enjoy!" Silence. Nobody spoke. I was not sure what to say either. What would you have said?

It's important to address this issue of bias. There are some who feel it doesn't matter what we teach and there are others who would like to have everything removed that is questionable. There are some who want Merchant of Venice and Othello withdrawn. I have some other thoughts on that. There are certainly some texts which do so much damage that they should be withdrawn.

In my view, <u>Little Black Sambo</u> is one of them. However,
placing a text in its historical and social contexts
would be one way of helping students to address the
question of bias. The notes I have enclosed on bias
should give you some ideas and this mini-unit on
Othello might give you some new approaches. Let me
know what you think.

     But if we are to help students we need to under-
stand how biased books and films work. We often talk
about bias as though it were a static mysterious
element in a film or book which makes it inherently
unsuitable.

     I'm sure you have observed that there is never
consensus on which books are biased and which are not.
What may be considered biased today may be acceptable
tomorrow.   This does not mean that we should abandon
the effort of providing our students with healthy
images of the world and of sharpening their abilities
to identify the demeaning depictions of groups of
people on the basis of their race and culture. No.
Each of us must address the bias of our times. Indeed
the bias in a novel or film works because of its
relationship to ideas and concrete relationships which
exist in certain times and societies.

     This triangle will give you a picture of the
relationships I have in mind

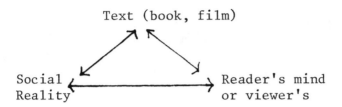

As members of society we have beliefs about groups
of people: their characteristics and their abilities
to perform and to fill certain social roles. Sometimes
social reality validates our beliefs. I can hear you
asking, "Why is Enid giving me all of this talk about
beliefs, and abilities and realities?" Yes, this
complexity cries out for illustration so here is one
from your school.

I was walking through the foyer the other day and
I noticed a photograph of the school basketball team.
All of the players were Black. "So what?" you might
ask. Everyone knows that they are natural when it
comes to physical things. Really! You might even
observe that considering the school population in
general and in the Black population in the school,
the Black students are over-represented on the team.
But the major question is why does this happen? Is it
really because blacks are better at physical things
or is it that historically sport was one area in which
they were allowed to participate and that they were
barred from other economic activities. Out of the
concrete situation developed cultural patterns and

traditions that have become associated with an
inherent quality of Blacks. This situation has helped
to shape the stereotypes of Blacks. In turn this
contributes to forcing them in the same kind of
activity. It is very complicated, but we need to be
able to get the bottom of things in order to change
them.

I can anticipate your argument that surely an
artist, or a writer isn't really concerned with this
kind of conspiracy I am suggesting here. Writers often
tell you that they write about what is out there and
that's about it.

No! No! I have to protest. An artist, author,
film maker has choices when he/she creates anything.
Depending on the framework a writer can choose to
reinforce biases or to try to change them. So the
author picks up stereotypes which are at large in the
society and we as readers or viewers bring to the text
a certain knowledge of the world in our heads which we
have developed partly from other films and books and
partly from looking at the situations of social
inequalities that exist in the world. With these
mental pictures at work we approach the text and have
our biases overtly or implicitly confirmed or rejected.
So biases work in text because they reflect some social
realities and they fit already held views.

I hope you see how these three points of my
triangle are related. There are three points of
attack when we are dealing with bias - the text, the
mind and the world. Now granted that we cannot get
at them all at once, we must still recognize the three-
pronged attack, if we are going to get to the bottom
of bias at least in our time. We have to keep
struggling to change unequal relationships in society,
those which keep certain groups in their places in that
society. At the same time we have to develop anti-
racist images of the world to give new messages and
then of course we must examine our own thinking. We
have to examine those things, especially those ideas,
assumptions, beliefs, reasons which helped us to make
sense of the world to this point.

So far I have spoken of bias as something negative. It is reasonable to wonder what makes something
negative or otherwise. By negative, I mean any
portrayal either visual or linguistic that invites
the interpretation that certain groups of people are
inherently inferior while others are superior and
that peoples' poverty and low status are their own
fault and not related in any way to the social system
in which they live.

All of this applies not only to material we
select and present but things the kids select. How
do we handle a situation in which we give a student
permission to select a book for something like
Uninterrupted Silent Reading and while making a routine

check we find that the sexism of a major character is
not to our liking. What do we do? Do we deselect
the book and tell the student he has to choose another
one? We worry about what the parents might think of
the school for allowing the student to read a book
which does not reflect their values. But what about
the credibility gap you are creating. Will the students
believe you next time you tell them they can select any
book? Worse still will they believe anything at all
which you tell them? And what if the book presents
people in a subordinate position on the grounds of race
and that view is never challenged. Besides how do we
know what their parents will and will not accept? And
are we going to censure books that promote violence in
various forms? These are the tough ones but not too
tough for us to try to answer them. And the toughest
one of all is what happens when we try to change the
books and kids get angry and act out. In one classroom
where a teacher attempted to change things and introduce
new texts some kids felt singled out and others felt
attacked and guilty.

Each of us will answer from our experience. I
hope some of the information in this book will
inform our answers.

Sincerely,

Enid

M. Bruun-Meyer

Jean Pierre Lacroix

Racism.
The Child Crippler

SELECTING RESOURCES

Activities

1. What's Behind the Words and Pictures?

Each member of the group will select material relevant to his or her subject area and apply the criteria provided below. The findings can be shared with the group.

THE PROCESS OF IDENTIFYING BIAS

Since authors convey their intentions both by what they include and exclude in terms of language and illustrations, these should be the focus of any assessment of material.

You should be aware of the impact of certain isolated expressions and illustrations in a text and of the sum of these expressions and illustrations in the total work. Areas of concern include:

1. Are certain words and illustrations systematically associated with specific groups of people?

2. Are groups of people frequently limited to certain jobs and activities?

3. How do authors and illustrators account for people's situations in life, and social problems in general?

4. What value judgments regarding personal worth are conveyed?

5. Is there implicit bias through the omission of groups of people who might have been included, given the setting?

In general, does the author deny the right to human dignity and the development of potential on grounds of race, culture, sex, ability, age, or social class?

Apply these questions to the material you are about to use in your classroom and see what you find.

2. What Am I Doing?

ASSESSMENT OF SELF, STUDENT, AND SITUATION

In order to make effective use of material which may be biased, you must assess not only the material, but also yourself, your students, and your teaching situations.

Questions for Self-Assessment

1. How do I feel about discussing the issue of racism? Are there situations in which discussions on race have made me feel uncomfortable? What has been the source of my discomfort?

2. How far can I control myself and the situation if students express views which differ sharply from mine?

3. What do I say if students begin to make racist comments?

4. How will I deal with controversial topics arousing negative reactions?

Some Approaches

1. Recognize that you will probably feel uncomfortable about the issue of racism. The discomfort is not a negative thing. To help you bring it to the surface, list some of the situations in which you have experienced discomfort around the issue of racism.

2. Let students know why statements are considered racist and also let them know the school's position on it.

3. Point out to students that discussions of racism may lead to unpleasantness, but that it is necessary to begin with these feelings.

4. Make a list of approaches which your colleagues have used in these situations.

M. Bruun-Meyer

3. How Are The Kids Getting Along?

Questions for Student Assessment:

1. To what extent have the students' life experiences prepared them for discussing this material?

2. What other material on this issue have the students studied?

3. What has been the focus of these books, films, etc.?

4. To what extent will this material broaden the students' understanding of the issue?

5. How far will this material confirm for the students an over-generalized view of a particular group of people, etc.?

6. If students identify personally with characters in the book or film, and feel they are being singled out, how might they react?

An Approach

The answers to these questions can be found by examining day books in order to see what the students have been viewing and reading. In addition, reflection or casual comments made by the students in other classes should provide some idea of how the students might react.

R. Rosenstock

4.   What's Going On In My School?

Questions for Assessment of School Situation:

1.   How far will current events in the school facilitate the examination of issues in the material?

2.   To what extent will current community sentiment facilitate the effective use of the material?

3.   Are there activities taking place in the school which will facilitate the examination of issues in the material, e.g., special assemblies, guest speakers, Black History Month, focus on the Holocaust?

4.   Have there been any incidents on the playing field, in the cafeteria or elsewhere which may relate to the issue in this material?

5.   Will current events, and the situation in the community facilitate the examination of the issues in the material?

The above questions might be discussed collectively in the community in order to develop an overall sense of the racial climate in the school and community.

5.   Critical Viewing

Select any of the films which the members of the group might be using for their classes and apply the criteria provided below.

GUIDELINES FOR CRITICAL VIEWING

1. Remember that every film-maker works within a particular framework. In other words, he/she has a set of assumptions about the way in which things ought to happen in life, and explanations for why things happen in life. Any framework, set of assumptions, or explanations must exclude other frameworks, assumptions and explanations. In this sense, then, every film has a bias. When we do not accept the bias of a particular work, we tend to describe the film as biased. Your task as a viewer is to detect the framework and general bias of the film-maker. As viewers, we think some biases are more human than others. In Canada's multicultural, multiracial society, we view as human, those biases which confirm the essential and equal humanity of all people.

2. Ask yourself: through whose ears and eyes are the scenes being experienced? Whose point of view are we being given in the various sequences?

3. Why do people have certain experiences in the film? How are events explained? For example, do things happen to people because they are either good or bad, right or wrong, lazy or industrious, or is it because of situations beyond their control?

4. What are you seeing in this film?

5. Who or what is in the background, and foreground of the various sequences in the film?

6. What is the relationship between sequences in the film? Do you notice contrasts and similarities between the sequences?

7. Who speaks in the film? Who is silent?

8. What does the music in the film make you think of? Significance of symbols?

9. What is omitted from the film?

10. How are your expectations of the film influencing what you are seeing and feeling about the film? For example, how is your experience with Hollywood influencing what you are seeing?

11. What would have to be different in the text of the film for the film to end differently?

EXAMINING A COURSE DESCRIPTION

Activities

1.   What is the Bias Here?

Read the following Course Description and identify the biases in it. As a staff you might like to examine all the course descriptions in the school and change any of them with anti-human biases.

Course Description
EURASIAN GEOGRAPHY — EUROPE AND ASIA   GEO 231

Area of Study: •Social and Environmental Studies
                                        Canadian Studies

Prerequisite: None

For a Canadian student, the study of geography of Eurasia offers an opportunity to investigate the fascinating variety of different people and places that make up the world's largest continent. The struggling and crowded masses of South Asia, the successful Japanese, and the highly advanced Western Europeans all provide highly interesting examples of people with a different approach to life from we Canadians.

A wide variety of resources such as films, maps, games and case studies will be utilized to help make the study of the various environments and cultures realistic and timely.

Questions to consider

(a)   Who is Canadian?

(b)   What would it mean to describe Canadians as "fascinating"?

(c)   What constitutes success?

(d)   What is the purpose of a course description?

SELECTING RESOURCES

Activities

1. Happy Birthday Dilroy

Students read the poem and try to answer the question Dilroy asks his mother in the poem.

John Agard
I Din Do Nuttin

HAPPY BIRTHDAY, DILROY

My name is Dilroy
I'm a little black boy
and I'm eight today.
My birthday cards say
it's great to be eight
and they sure right
coz I got a pair of skates
I want for a long long time.
My birthday cards say,
Happy Birthday, Dilroy!
**But, Mummy, tell me why
they don't put a little boy
that looks a bit like me.
Why the boy on the card so white?**

2. Students select a number of books from the library and conduct a survey in order to determine the racial make-up of the characters and the roles played by the different characters. Their checklist could include the following:—

    1. Is the race and/or the culture of the characters mentioned?

    2. What are people of different races doing if they are included at all?

    3. Who has been omitted who might have been included?

    4. What overall message does the author give about people of different races?

Activities

Secondary

1. A Unit on Othello for Secondary Students

1. Students can listen to or read the play *Othello*. Working in groups, they select several passages in which Othello and Desdemona are described, e.g. Act I, Scene i, lines 85-170. In the discussion, students might consider the following:

    (a) Who is the speaker in each case?

    (b) What do we know about the speaker which might influence his/her point of view with regard to Othello and Desdemona?

    (c) How would you classify the words used to describe Othello and Desdemona?

    (d) How would you account for the differences in the descriptions of both characters?

2. Members of the class listen to or read Act I of the play, paying special attention to what characters say about Brabantio and also what he reveals about himself. The class discusses the character of Brabantio exploring the following questions:

    (a) How is he viewed by other citizens?

    (b) What is his social standing?

    (c) How would you explain his attitude to Othello on the night of the marriage?

M. Bruun-Meyer

This description can lead into the topic of interracial and intercultural dating and marriage. Students can explore their feelings on this subject by examining the arguments made by the parents in the 4-H Club article and comparing them with those of Brabantio.

4-H WON'T VISIT SIX NATIONS RESERVE

A 4-H club in Manitoba cancelled an exchange with Ohsweken 4-H club after it found the Ontario members were Indians and that the Manitoba group would be staying on the Six Nations Reserve.

Theresa Harris, leader of the Ohsweken club, said the Manitoba club backed out of the exchange on Thursday after its leader found out that the Ohsweken participants were native Indians.

"Would you send your child to sleep with Indians?" Charlotte Hutton, leader of the 4-H club in Oak Lake, Man., said in a telephone interview from her home last night near Virden. "Would you sleep with Indians? You go and sit for seven days on that reserve and live with them...."

Asked why the Oak Lake group didn't want its members to participate in the exchange, Mrs. Hutton said: "I have lived beside the Oak Lake Reserve for 18 years and I know what goes on." She said she was upset because her group was "screened completely".

She became angry when asked if she was prejudiced against natives. "No, I am not prejudiced against Canadian Indians," she said forcefully. Asked if she liked Indians, the response was sarcastic: "I love them."

"They have their liquor problems," Phyllis Gumpf, mother of a teenage boy and girl in the Manitoba club, said from Mrs. Hutton's house. "They fight, and no way am I going to send my two kids there to be stabbed," she said vehemently.

When asked whether it was fair to let Indians on the Manitoba Reserve stand for other Indians, Mrs. Gumpf said: "They're all the same — you can't tell me any different. I'm not prejudiced, but I told my kids what they were up against and they said 'No way'."

The exchange, part of a federal Government program called Open House Canada, was to take place from July 26 to August 3. Fifteen members from each group ranging in age from 14 to 22 were to have taken part.

A letter from Ottawa confirming the exchange plans on March 12 reads in part: "The participants in the Open House Canada program agree that they shall not discriminate or permit any discrimination by reason of race, creed, sex or colour, nationality, ethnic origin, place of birth or language of participant.''

Mrs. Harris said the Ohsweken members were ''always brought up that we were all equal — so it (the cancellation) kind of hits them hard.''

After meeting the 15 participants and their parents last night, she said the group is drafting letters to Indian and Northern Affairs Minister, John Munro, the National Indian Brotherhood, the Manitoba Indian Brotherhood, the Union of Ontario Indians and the Human Rights Commission asking for support.

Ohsweken is located about 20 kilometres southeast of Brantford and Oak Lake is about the same distance west of Brandon.

Christine McLaren
Globe & Mail, Saturday, June 18, 1980.

3. The teacher could contact a theatre group which has presented *Othello* and have students interview the actors. In preparation for this visit, students might consider the following questions:

   (a) How far does the issue of race influence the actors' interpretation of their parts?

   (b) Is there any difference in the effect of the performance if the actor playing Othello is a Black person or if he is made-up to take on the appearnce of a Black person?

   (c) To what extent does the resolution of the play depend on the fact that Othello is a Black man, and that Desdemona is a white woman?

   (d) How far are Black actors limited in the roles they play in a predominantly white society?

4. This class attempts a modern version of *Othello* with an ending which differs from the one in the original play. They should be invited to examine their reasons for attributing certain actions and words to different characters. It should be brought to their attention if they replace old stereotypes with new ones.

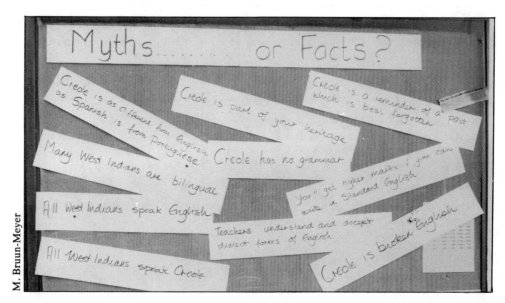

M. Bruun-Meyer

Discuss the following table and have students generate their own list of positive and negative connotations of words in different subject areas.

LANGUAGE IS NOT NEUTRAL				
Concept	**Positive Connotation**	**Context**	**Negative Connotation**	**Context**
1. A piece of cloth worn as a garment	Clothing	The skirt of a North American woman	Costume	The sari of an Indian woman
2. Small dwelling of simple construction	Cottage	A shepherd's house in the Scottish hills	Hut	House of an African villager

Concept	Positive Connotation	Context	Negative Connotation	Context
3. System of institutional-ized expres-sions of sacred beliefs, obser-vances and social practices found within a given cultural context	Religion	Christianity	Superstition	African religions e.g. Animism
4. Taking the initiative, being bold and self-confident	Assertive	Male executive	Aggressive	Female executive
5. Battle in which one side side practically eliminates the opponent	Victory	The Europeans conquering the Native people	Massacre	The Native People conquering the Europeans
6. State inter-vention in social upheaval	Maintaining law and order	British police-men quelling rioters	Introducing repressive meaures	Polish govern-ment dealing with strikers
7. People engaged in liberation struggles	Freedom Fighters	Resistance Movement in France	Terrorists	Pre-indepen-dence period in Zimbabwe

Resources

Black History: Lost, Stolen or Strayed (2 parts)
16mm film 54 mins.

Bill Cosby highlights the participation of Black people in the cultural and economic development of North American society. In his exploration he demonstrates the systematic exclusion of Black people in the recorded history of the country.

Available: Ministry of Citizenship and Culture.

More Than Bows and Arrows
16mm film 56 mins.

A film portraying Indian and Inuit contributions to the development of North American government, environmental use and other important areas of life.

Available: Ministry of Citizenship and Culture.

Myself, Yourself
16mm film 30 mins.

Five racial minorities discuss their experiences of school life from the viewpoint of being always excluded from the curriculum. The film highlights the potential of curriculum for shaping a child's social identity.

Available: National Film Board Offices

4 STUDENT SERVICES:
How Anti-Racist are Yours?

M. Bruun-Meyer

"The kids are so low! They just don't have the ability!"

"I used to think so too until I began to assess them differently."

Guidance Counselor and
Classroom Teacher

Dear M,

So one of the representatives from a highly "academic" school came to talk to the grade eights in a school near to yours. As the kids were filing into the hall, one Black student who is known for mouthing off to teachers was grabbed by the guidance counsellor and asked just where he thought he was going. He made it very clear to the youngster that there was no way that he could ever go to that type of school. He was told to return to his classroom. This student whom we will call Richard for the time being was not his usual self. He is not one for tears but this time he wept openly. His home room teacher inquired and she was told what had happened. She was truly indignant about this and went straight to the principal. The principal spent some time talking with the guidance counsellor. Apparently their conversation was not a pleasant one, for the guidance counsellor was seen sulking around the school for the rest of the day. Richard was told that he could sit in on the session after all but he declined.

Now how did all of this happen? I gather that this guidance counsellor had worked with Richard and the other students before they came to their present school. In both cases the schools' populations were of low socio-economic background and this teacher had always prided himself on knowing how to deal with "those types" as he often described them.

The guidance counsellor's former association with Richard and students from Richard's background probably influenced his comment. But more fundamental to the issue are some views that are commonly held about ability and performance. We tend to confuse both. We have certainly developed the tools in education to measure a student's performance but do we really know that we are measuring what the student is able to do? The other influence here is with our attitude towards ability. We often speak of it as though it were static and had no possibility of it being developed. This is part and parcel of what I call the rhetoric of limitation -- the measure which tells you how far you are going to stop even before you start. That in part must have influenced the guidance counsellor's performance, even though he himself may not be aware of this.

    Finally, this guidance counsellor was probably
responding to a commonly held stereotype about the
potential of black students. We seem to have working
images of which students do which sort of activities.
I am sure that for every ethnic and racial group you
could associate certain abilities and characteristics.
Stereotypes develop as we attempt to organize people
into categories and to make sense of our world. That
in itself is not the problem. However we are in real
trouble when these categories are so closed that they
prevent us from seeing people's full potential. I
think the guidance counsellor was suffering from that.
By the way, we really have to give credit to the
principal and teacher for acting so decisively.

                  Sincerely,

ASSESSMENT AND PLACEMENT

(Activities)

1. Response to the letter

Read the letter and jot down initial reactions. Reflect on the roles of the guidance counsellor, the principal, the teacher, and the student. What might each have emphasized if they were recounting the incident? What action might you have taken had you been a member of the staff? Share your responses with the other members of the group. Facilitator should draw people's attention to the beliefs and assumptions which their responses appear to reflect.

2. Abiiity and Performance — A Brainstorming Session

Engage the group in a brainstorming session on the concept of ability and performance. List their responses to the following questions:

1. Is ability inherent?

2. Can ability be developed?

3. What kinds of abilities do society and school value?

4. What kinds of abilities do you value?

5. Are all kinds of abilities distributed equally among all racial and cultural groups?

6. What, if any, is the relationship between performance and ability?

3. Review of Assessment Tools

Conduct a survey of the initial assessment procedures in your school. Some questions to consider:

1. Who is responsible for Initial Assessment of new students?

2. What support is provided to this person to allow him/her to perform this duty (reduced teaching load; cover for class)?

3. Are interpreters involved in the cases of non-English speaking students?

4.   Who receives the information from the assessment?

5.   What mechanisms are in place to monitor the relationship between assessment information and program provided for the student?

6.   How often is the assessment reviewed?

4.   Assess Yourself

Select some of the assessment tools developed by your department, school, board or ministry and examine them for their implications in a multicultural/multiracial/multi-social-class school. Here is an example of a self-assessment tool for teachers based on very laudable criteria from the *Language Across the Curriculum*, Ministry of Education Document, 1978. It is possible to follow these guidelines and still unintentionally discriminate against minority students. Next to them, I have listed the racial and cultural factors which must be considered if you are to provide equality of opportunity for children of all racial and cultural backgrounds. From: *Appendix A: Evaluation Checklists for Teachers*, p. 17.

Self-Evaluation Ministry Criteria	Further Consideration
1. Is my questioning thoughtfully prepared to foster higher thinking skills (application, analysis, synthesis, evaluation)?	Do I unconsciously direct more complex, thoughtful questions to some students and not to others? If this is the case, is there a particular racial or cultural breakdown to the groups? If so, is it because they have had difficulty with these kinds of questions? If this is the case, what remedial steps have I taken?
2. Do I encourage critical thinking and response?	How far am I willing to allow response which reflects values which diverge sharply from mine? What if the student's response seems to be asserting a racial and cultural pride which may be different from my own? What if the

Self-Evaluation Ministry Criteria	Further Consideration
	response implies that Canada is a racist country and that racism exists in the school? When do I begin to feel defensive?
3. Do my students feel free to take risk with language (use new words, guess at meanings, attempt new structures and styles)?	What have I done to create a positive environment in my room to foster the confidence necessary for risk-taking? Have I tried to be responsive to the language of those who have an accent or some vocabulary items different from mine (e.g. West Indian speakers of Standard English)? How have I attempted to confirm and accept those students and their culture so that they trust me enough to take risks in my classroom?
4. Do I assist the students when dealing with material of gradually increasing difficulty, to set purposes, to relate the material **to their** experiences, to unlock the meaning of key words or phrases and thus to gain confidence?	How much do I know of the experiences of students from racial and cultural minorities? How often have I legitimized the experience of those students in the process of my teaching so that they recognize that their experiences count and are acceptable for regular classroom use not just on multicultural days?
5. Do I encourage my students to evaluate their discussions and increase their awareness of group dynamics?	Do I ever encourage the students to examine whether racial and cultural differences hinder the group discussions and make them, perhaps, less open to ideas of a group member of another colour?

M. Bruun-Meyer

ASSESSMENT AND PLACEMENT

While it is recognized that students do not participate directly in their assessment and placement, their lives are affected most directly by it. These are issues of interest to students, which are connected to the larger concern of assessment and placement — that is, the way it is experienced.

Activities

1. Read the letter to Marcia to the class and encourage them to discuss how the student might have felt in this situation. Have them rewrite the letter from the student's point of view. Suggest that they include why they think the injustice took place.

Elementary

Activities

1. Arrange a trip for students to another school in the Board and learn how that school is different from, or the same as, theirs. They might check out the following areas:

   1. What are the pictures like in this school?

   2. Are there carpets on the floor?

   3. Does the school have computers?

   4. Who attends the school — gender, race, culture?

   5. How large are their classes?

   6. How old is the school?

   After writing their findings, students might explore the reasons for the similarities and differences.

2. Arrange for students to see the film, *Black History: Lost, Stolen or Strayed.* Discuss the ways in which our images of people are partly produced by the media. Encourage the students to examine the extent to which those stereotypes still exist.

Secondary

CAREER COUNSELLING

Activities

Elementary

1. Taking Stock

Students prepare a questionnaire for a survey to be conducted in the community. From the survey they should be able to determine the criteria managers use for hiring.

Questions for the Manager:

1. What do you look for in the people whom you hire?

2. How and where do you advertise?

3. Do you find it easier to have certain groups work for you, e.g. men vs women, Chinese vs Blacks?

Students need to survey the following places

—Banks

—Police Station

—School

—Restaurant

Who works there?

Age — middle aged, teenagers

Gender — men, women

Racial background — white, South Asian, Chinese

Who does what?

Do the men do certain kinds of work?

What are they?

Who is the manager?

Who deals with the public?

Who is giving instructions?

How many of the caretakers are women?

How many of the secretaries are men?

How many of the teaching and administrative staff in your school belong to the same racial group as 1/3 of the students or 1/2 of the student body?

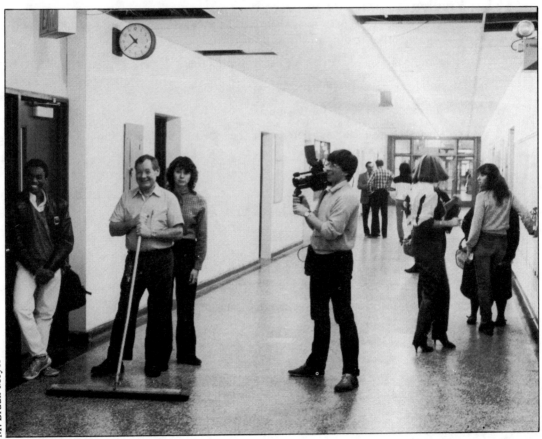

M. Bruun-Meyer

Secondary

Activities

1. Choosing a Career

Invite the class to develop scenarios from their experiences of being counselled into taking certain courses or pursuing certain career goals. Have them role play these scenarios and explore their feelings in the process. The video tape, *Message From the Classroom* which specifically deals with counselling might be used as a stimulus here. Have them compare their scenarios with the ones in the video tape.

2. Finding Answers for Excuses

Invite the students to explore answers for the following statements which are frequently made in order to defend current hiring practices.

1. No more hiring so, of course, we can't change this.

2. The unions oppose Affirmative Action so what can we do?

3. No minorities ever apply for the jobs.

4. We always choose the best person for the job — we're not going to choose someone just because she is Chinese.

Resources

Message from the Classroom: A Student's View of Racism
2 video cassettes 36 mins. and 35 mins.

The first of these tapes explores racial stereotyping and academic streaming through scenarios developed by high school students in Toronto. The dramatizations of the experience are followed by a lively and enlightened discussion on the part of the students.

Available: Cross Cultural Communication Centre and the Toronto Board of Education.

Only My Best Will Do
Video cassette 20 mins.

This is a sequel to the video, **Be A Good Boy Now**. It depicts the experience of racism faced by a young Jamaican student who moves to Canada. It is particularly instructive to listen to his teachers in Canada assess his ability, his performance and his possibility of making it in Canada.

Available at the Ministry of Citizenship and Culture.

CONCLUSION

Hi Enid,

I've just finished reading your letters to me and I must tell you first of all, how pleased I am that you followed up on my suggestion to use letters to share your ideas with teachers. Nothing makes a teacher more pleased than seeing her ideas taken seriously.

It's also very encouraging to discover that we are doing some things right. Sometime ago, we surveyed the parents in our school on a number of issues and the Grade 9 English class made an orientation handbook for new parents. In fact, some of the suggested activities are done quite regularly, but you have shown how they might also be related to race and culture.

I think you know that I always get a little
concerned when we discuss bias and books. It's so
close to the issue of censorship, and once we start
book-banning; there's no telling where it will stop.
In any case, I am going to have a look at Othello and
Merchant of Venice and see if we can make positive
use of those classics.

The section on student services has made me think
about the differences between the two secondary
schools in which I have taught. We had very different
expectations for those two sets of students. One
group was heading to the best universities in Ontario
and the other, well, who knows? The two school
buildings said a lot about the direction of the
students too. One looked a little like the Ontario
Science Centre; the other was dark and depressing
and needed a coat of paint.

In those days when you worked in my classroom,
you used to ask for feedback. You never seemed to
mind hearing when some of your ideas were a little
off the wall. There are a couple places in the guide
when I think you are out to lunch, especially where
you ask so much of teachers. Sometimes you forget
that some of us work in schools where we get little
support for new ideas. You have also forgotten the
price tag attached to some of these ideas. You should
have included a section on how to get the people with
the money to fund these activities. But knowing you,
you probably have this in mind for your next book!

In the meantime, you can take some comfort in the fact that this book will be helpful in a number of ways. For one thing, the issue of racism will be more readily examined in staff room talk and in professional development workshops. And speaking of workshops, I attended one the other day when we were being talked at about having "the proper attitude" towards students of all ethnic backgrounds. It was one of those 45 minute sessions when we were expected to understand everything about prejudice and discrimination. I am beginning to have very grave doubts about this mickey-mouse approach to serious topics. This guide does make claims for a complex approach to the subject of racism. But I can hear you saying, "Marcia, we have to use all the time we have. We can whet their appetites and hope they ask for more".

Well, Letters To Marcia does make me ask for more. I feel I want more for my students and for myself. It gives me some sense of optimism for my profession and perhaps even some hope for a just Canadian society. It suggests some places to start and that's always helpful.

You haven't heard the last of me yet. I'll be in touch again.

Sincerely,

Marcia